JOURNEY INTO DAWN

By the Same Author

WHITE FIRE
SILVER IN THE SUN
FLAME IN THE WIND
MISS HUMPETY COMES TO TEA
LIGHT OF THE YEARS
THIS GOLDEN SUMMIT
THE RADIANT QUEST
SPLENDOR AHEAD
FACING THE STARS
SOME BRIGHTER DAWN
BETWEEN ETERNITIES
THE LIFTED LAMP
THE WIND-SWEPT HARP
THE CRYSTAL FOUNTAIN
APPLES OF GOLD
SONGS FOR COURAGE
SONGS OF FAITH
SONGS OF HOPE
SONGS FOR COMFORT
BRIGHT HARVEST

Journey
INTO DAWN

By
GRACE NOLL CROWELL

HARPER & BROTHERS, PUBLISHERS
New York

Library of Congress catalog card number: 55-8520

To Norman
IN MEMORIAM

¶ Credit is due the following publications for permission to reprint certain poems in this book.

Pilgrim Press
Methodist Publications
The Christian Advocate
The Christian Herald
Baptist Publications
Unity
Message
D.C. Cook Co.
The Lutheran
Progressive Farmer
Washington Star

CONTENTS

JOURNEY INTO DAWN   13

THERE WILL BE LIGHT   14

THE HORIZON   15

LAND OF THE EVER YOUNG   16

THE LEAST OF THESE   17

OUT OF THE DARK   19

FOREST SANCTUARY   20

SUMAC   21

ROADWAY IN SEPTEMBER   22

THE CRAFTSMAN   23

WORKER IN WOOD   24

THE HOLY LAND   25

HE WAS SO YOUNG   27

YOUTHFUL DAVID   28

YOUNG SCULPTOR   29

AN OLD HYMN   30

LIVING WITH HEARTBREAK   31

FRUITS OF THE VALLEY   32

UNWELCOME GUESTS   33

"WITH WINGS AS EAGLES"   34

A STORMY SEA   36

A Voice from the Alamo 37
From a Desert Place 38
Color 39
Birches in Spring 41
Understanding 42
Silence 43
The Poet and the Architect 44
A Darkened Street 45
The Essence 46
Ancient Materials 47
While It Is Early 48
Evening at Emmaus 49
Since You Are Gone 51
Star in the Darkness 52
Red Tree 53
Winter Fields 54
Deer at Evening 55
The Wild Colt 56
Sagebrush 57
Mountain Torrent 58
A Voice Rang Out 59
We Met the Christ 60
Autumn Fires 61
If Christmas Be Kept 62
In the Church of the Holy
  Sepulcher 63

To a Lady in Black   65
Organ and Choir   66
"Our Father"   67
The Harpist   68
Unuttered Faith   69
Walking in Rain   70
Compassion   71
To a Christian Doctor   72
When Sleep Is a Stranger to
    My Eyes   73
Spanish Song   74
Anomaly   75
Ocean Sunset   76
Two Old Friends   77
The Brave Doing of the
    Common Task   78
I Wish I Knew   79

JOURNEY INTO DAWN

Journey Into Dawn

I HAVE traveled through the dark,
I have traveled far,
With no moon to light my way,
And without a star
To pierce the darkness and to show
Me clearly how to go.

I have traveled toward the dawn—
Always toward the dawn.
Well I knew the light would break
If I journeyed on;
But the dark was deep, ah me,
In its intensity!

Then suddenly the East was lit,
Was lit with hope and light.
Weary I was, and worn I was,
But the long dark night
Lay like a shadow long since past—
And the dawn was there at last!

There Will Be Light

GOD does not leave his children without
    light.
        He saw that light was good, and so he
keeps
The silver lamp of stars lit in the night,
The moon's soft radiance while mankind sleeps.
Never a cloud so dense but some faint ray
Marks where the sun moves out beyond the dark;
And I have found that never a night or day,
If I but search, there is some little spark
Of brilliance permeating any fog:
Some home-sweet lamp set on a heavenly sill,
A searchlight lifting through the city's smog,
A guiding beacon glowing on a hill.
"Let there be light—and there was light." O men,
Even in this dark hour there is a light
Waiting beyond the clouds to shine again:
The lifted lamp of God, full-orbed and bright,
Still burns despite our anxious fears and doubt,
A light that never will be blackened out.

The Horizon

LIFE is immortal, and love is immortal,"
      With assurance one speaks, and another
      makes reply:
"Then tell me, what is death?" and comes the
      answer:
"Death is the horizon, joining earth and sky.
And it is nothing, O anxious heart, it is nothing,
It is a mirage that moves through the shimmering
      light,
It is the continuation of a journey,
It is but the limitation of our sight."

And I who have the need of consolation
Am comforted to know that life moves on
With never a frightening moment of cessation,
With never an endless night without a dawn.
Open our eyes, Lord God, that we may see
Past the horizon into Eternity.

Land of the Ever Young

IN AN old Celtic legend Heaven is called
"Tir nan Og"—the Land of the Ever Young.
Oh, beautiful beyond our brightest dreams,
Oh, sweeter than any song that has been sung
Is the vision called up by the pictured words:
Where age can never enter a domain,
Nor sorrow lay its hand upon the heart,
Nor weariness beset, nor tears, nor pain.

Land of the Ever Young—the ever green
Country of the blest sends out its light:
A promise whose fulfillment will be kept,
A beacon lifted high before our sight,
A call whose essence is the living truth,
That bids us seek and find eternal Youth.

The Least of These

OUTSIDE the wind was cold, the snow
  deep-piled,
    And to my door there came a weeping
child
Scantily clothed and hungering to be fed,
And I whom fire and food had comforted
Could not withhold that comfort, so I bade
The child come in and share the food I had.
I brought warm raiment as he sought the flame,
And lo, my eyes blurred, and the child became
A man! I saw his reaching hands were scarred
From the print of nails, and that his brow was
    marred
From the crown of thorns that one day he had
    worn.
The shadow of the cross that he had borne
Darkened behind him . . . "Master, Lord!" I
    cried,
Amazed and breathless, coming to his side—
"Yea, child," he said, as I fell on my knees,

"What ye have done for one of the least of these
Ye have done for me." Then suddenly he was
gone,
But his clear words forever will sound on.

Out of the Dark

I SHALL follow the footsteps of those gone
        before me:
The brave, courageous ones who have found
    their way
Out of the dark by facing the sunrising
Of a new day.

They, too, had an unseen Presence close beside
        them;
They, too, must have found the dark hills steep
        and high;
And yet they did not falter in their going,
And neither shall I.

As day broke for them, surely it will be breaking
Upon this strangely dark and troubled night—
Look—Look yonder! Far on the east horizon—
The Light! The Light!

Forest Sanctuary

(I Chronicles 16:33)

"THEN shall the trees of the wood sing
out
At the presence of the Lord," 'tis said.
Here in this wood I hear the shout
From the waving treetops overhead:
A hallelujah chorus sung
From boughs tossed by a lifting breeze,
As if a gladness had been wrung
From the roots, the trunks, the leaves of trees.

The presence of the Lord is here
Within this emerald solitude.
If one but listen he can hear
Through organ pipes and cello wood
Music lifting from the sod
Where the trees of the wood sing out to God.

Sumac

BEAUTY in death!
   Beauty beyond believing!
   Why then the catching breath,
The bitter grieving?

The sumac is dead, quiet and slow
   the dying,
Yet never a redder red
On the hillside lying;

Never a warmer gleam
In a hearthfire ember . . .
This is a dream to dream,
And to remember.

Roadway in September

THE heat glimmers down on the long white
        road
    Where the latent strength of the sun is
  spent,
While out of each splash of shadow and shade
The chill of the winter's breath is sent.
The wild rose berries hold crimson light,
The asters burn through the autumn day,
And down through the shimmering thistle mist
Gay butterflies dip in fantastic play.

Oh, familiar the rustle of ripened corn,
And the sound of the pop of the milkweed pod,
And sweet is the scent of the honeyed air
From the fields where the clover heads toss and
        nod.
And deep in my heart is a tenderness
For the girl and her lover who walk in the glow
Of the September sun, as we used to walk,
O Lover of mine in the long ago.

The Craftsman

THE Master hewed a table leg,
    The Master carved a yoke,
    And to everyone who came to him
I am certain that he spoke
Of vital and eternal things,
And when they went away
They carried more than his handiwork
Into the blue-gold day.

They carried wonder in their hearts,
And hope they had not had;
They marveled at him, and new faith
Sprang up to make them glad.

O Master of us common folk,
We need to seek your shop,
To hear your calm voice speaking clear
The while your skilled hands stop
Their woodcraft labor as you give
Triumphant words by which to live.

Worker with Wood

JESUS who worked long with wood
  Must have found all lumber good,
  Must have loved a board's bright length
With its fine resilient strength,
Must have loved to send his plane
Smoothly, swiftly down the grain:
Grain that time long gone had made
Beautiful through sun and shade.

How he must have loved the shine
Of a golden length of pine,
And delighted in the glow
Of red cedar! Oh, we know
That the shavings at his feet
Falling there must have been sweet
As the fragrance of the dawn
On the hills of Lebanon.
It was blessed, it was good
For our Lord to work with wood.

The Holy Land

I AM sure today that I can see
Christ's footsteps in this golden sand,
And every sail on Galilee
Is being guided by his hand.
I mark the pathways through the grass
Where surely once his sandals trod;
The wild flowers, bending as I pass,
Once bowed before the Son of God.

The wheat fields out from Bethlehem
Are golden now, and cool and sweet;
I see the twelve, and he with them,
Plucking the kerneled grain to eat.
I cannot pass a wayside well
But I can see him at its brink,
And a woman hurrying to tell
Of the living water there to drink.

He leads me and I follow on
Humbly and with bated breath.
I cross the plains of Esdraelon,
I tread the streets of Nazareth;

I climb Mount Carmel, and behold
The blue, blue Mediterranean lies
A quiver of scarlet, blue and gold
Beneath the colored evening skies.

Surely a young lad often came
Out from the town to climb this hill,
To view within the sunset flame
The clear lights that are burning still.
Mount Tabor and Mount Hermon raise
Their lofty snow-clad summits there,
As I recall how many days
He sought a mountain's peace for prayer.

Over every traveled hallowed place
I search for him, and I have seen
His reaching hands, his form, his face:
For Christ still walks in Palestine.

He Was So Young

HE WAS so young the while he walked the
     earth:
    Thirty and three years, all too swiftly
flown.
He had no home, no roof, no glowing hearth,
No little child that he could call his own,
And yet the whole wide world was his—his love
For all mankind, a passion in his breast,
The sky his roof, and he was mindful of
Each little child that came at his behest.

Thirty and three years—burning like a flame
For righteousness, for justice and for truth,
A life summed up in one immortal name
To etch its imprint on the hearts of Youth.
For he was young, and ever will be young,
He is one with all the Youth of earth today.
O you who follow in his steps give tongue
In praise of him, your Comrade on the way.

Youthful David

YOUNG David was an expert
In two varied things:
The capturing of music
For his harp's taut strings,
And in the accurate casting
Of pebbles from his slings.

Two fine arts that the shining
Future was to claim:
Music to go lifting
Like a living flame,
Music that would one day
Perpetuate his name.

And his handmade slingshot,
With its swift release,
Was to seek a target
That a war might cease;
One small stone, God-guided,
To bring a nation peace!

Young Sculptor

HE STANDS before the marble block
That holds a wingéd dream, and he
The one whose gold key can unlock
The door and set the white dream free.
His eyes are burning coals of fire,
His hands are steady, sure and swift;
Born of the flame of his desire
Soon a beautiful thing will lift
Its white wings from the powdered dust
To stand serene with graceful ease:
A statue neither moth nor rust
Can mar throughout the centuries.
O young deliverer of a dream!
O Youth, with years left to be spent,
Radiant may your future gleam,
And great be your accomplishment.
Yours is a gift from God—your skill
A sacred trust you must fulfill.

An Old Hymn

MY HEART was heavy with an ancient
grief;
Life's fever had been running like a
fire—
The hurt left by it seemed beyond relief,
Then suddenly the voices of the choir
Joined with an organ's golden sound, and broke
Across the silence of the shadowed room,
Shattering it as if an angel spoke:
"Lead, kindly Light, amid the encircling
gloom . . ."

"So long thy power hath blessed me, sure it still
Will lead me on . . ." each lifted lovely word
Assured and comforted my heart until
My faith was quickened, and a new hope stirred.
O blessed kindly Light! O sweet release!
An old loved hymn has brought my spirit peace.

Living with Heartbreak

HOW many, ah, how many go their way
　　With heartbreak their companion on the
　　　road,
Keeping a secret that they never tell
Of sorrow that became too great a load
For any heart to bear! How brave they are,
These valiant conquerors of inward grief,
Who pause and smile and say that all is well,
And then move forward, brave beyond belief.

Living with heartbreak! Lord of the rugged road,
Be thou their comrade as they journey on,
Lighten the heavy darkness of their night,
Point out the signal of an early dawn.
Reward them for the hours, the days, the years
That they have borne their grief with unshed
　　tears.

Fruits of the Valley

OUT of the Valley of Waiting I have
brought
Fruit that was bittersweet to my thirsty
mouth.
Through many a darkly shadowed day I sought
Northward and eastward—to the west and south
For the gold and crimson globes that could light
the land
And give me sustenance as I journeyed on:
Globes that I could gather with my hand
And carry with me up the hillside dawn.

I found the trees that were heavy with the weight
Of the hanging fruit; I plucked them with much
care;
At first the acrid bitterness was great,
And the disappointment all that I could bear.
But now—ah, now—the shadowed valley past,
And the sunlit hills before my eager feet,
Strangely, I have found the fruit at last
Freed of its bitterness, and singularly sweet.

Unwelcome Guests

PAIN knows me well—he has often been my
      guest.
    I had not welcomed him, and yet he stayed
As one who meant to find a needed rest
With a table spread, and a clean bed smoothly
     made.

And once he brought with him another guest:
His name was "Sorrow," and I tried the more
To turn the key against them, tried my best,
But nothing barred their entrance to my door.

O strange unwelcome guests, I bade you go,
But looking backward through the lengthening
     years
I know you taught me much I did not know,
Although I learned my lessons through my tears.

I would not have you back—and yet—and yet—
You are the guests I never shall forget.

"With Wings as Eagles"

THE promise: "They that wait upon the
    Lord
    Shall renew their strength"
Is like a heartening shout from some high hill,
It rings across the centuries' far length
To bless the listening ones. The word is still
As precious and as true as it was when
It first was spoken to the hearts of men.

"They shall mount up with wings as eagles" and
    lo,
The earthbound pilgrims contemplate that flight
With hope renewed; and strengthened by that
    hope,
Prepare to meet and face the dazzling light
Of sun and moon and stars through boundless
    space,
When they shall mount with a golden eagle's
    grace.

"They shall run, and not be weary." Oh, to run

With all the high winds from the shores of
      heaven!
"They shall walk, and not faint." Ah, best of all
Is this great promise that the Lord has given
To the weary ones who long to walk upright,
Strengthened by his power and his might.

A Stormy Sea

TO UNDERSTAND how lengthened time
must be
Since the world began—look on a stormy
sea:
Its gray face furrowed by the plows of care,
Its foaming beard atoss, its thinned white hair
Whipped by the wind—pale light-revealing eyes
Lost to any wonder or surprise.
Worn with tumult, saddened by the years,
Its hollow cheeks adrip with salty tears,
It is as old as time itself—this wandering Jew
Whose troubled voyaging is never through.

Look on a stormy sea if you would know
Of ages far away and long ago.

A Voice from the Alamo

THIS is holy ground on which we stand,
This is where they stood when the mad
flood
Came boiling upward from a foreign land
To redden darkly with arterial blood:

With blood at a white heat that freedom might
Be as unsullied as new flags unfurled;
That the word might hold undimmed the radiant
light
Of hope for a perplexed and troubled world.

O men, could we, would we stand firm today
Before the certainty of coming doom?
Pray God that we would be as brave as they
Who fought and died in this small rock-lined
room.

Have we grown soft? God harden sinew, bone.
Before our danger may we come alive
To have one aim, one goal, one star alone
Called "Freedom," that our freedom may survive.

From a Desert Place

DESOLATE miles of sand, and a hot wind
blowing—
Only the yucca's candelabrums set
Deep in the swirling mounds, their gold flames
shaken,
And the stolid cacti beneath the wind's wild fret
Give signs of life, until a startled lizard
Skids to a flat green stop along the sand.
And yet despite this barrenness—sheer beauty
Lifts in this wide untrammeled desert land.

Strange how colorless miles draw daring color
From unseen sources that wield an unseen brush
To paint with vivid rose and strange wild purple
The low serrated wastes, and in the hush
One stands amazed and breathless with the
thought
Echoing from the past: "What hath God
wrought!"

Color

HAVE you noticed, have you seen
          That God loves green?
          And that he loves clear yellow, too,
And blue—blue!
The trees, the sky, the glint of the sun,
The million yellow flowers that run
Their windy way;
And God loves gray:
The mist, the rain, the clouds that fly
When storms go by.
And looking at the dawn, I think
That God loves pink.
But red—have you ever thought how he
Uses it so sparingly?
A red flower here, another there,
A red wing flashing on the air,
A cluster of berries on a limb—
Red must be jewel-like to him,
And very precious . . . but if I
Were asked the color I like best

'Twould be the color of the sky
Some autumn evening in the west:
Not mauve, not pink, not gold, not flame—
It has no name!

Birches in Spring

M ORNING—and young birches in the
spring:
Their jagged gold and green leaves
brightly thinned,
No mind could formulate a lovelier thing
Than these slim saplings swaying on the wind,
Shot through with light, their flecked white bark
agleam,
Their slender shadows slanted on the grass . . .
Here is the glorious substance of a dream,
Here is beauty only the blind could pass
Without the quick desire to kneel and pray
To the God who set these jewels in a day.

Understanding

BECAUSE I, too, have sorrowed, I can go
  The road, dear sorrowing one, that you now
    know.
The road is dark, but if we reach our hands
To touch the robe of One who understands,
The path will brighten as he guides us on
Into the breaking light of the new dawn.

Because I, too, have suffered, I can feel
The pain you bear, and know that God can heal
The deepest wound that any heart has borne.
He waits beside us, knowing we are worn
From sleepless nights and weary restless days.
Testing us, it may be, yet he stays
Close beside us until sweet release
Brings us the joyous blessedness of peace.

Silence

HOW silently the moments go,
    How still the hours pass—
    More quietly than winds that sweep
Across the meadow grass.

How very still the seasons move:
The winter, spring and fall—
They swing on hinges smoothly oiled,
And make no sound at all.

The moon is silent in its flight,
The stars' long nightly run
Is on still feet. There is no sound
Made by the journeying sun.

I think God loves tranquillity,
And silence; and I, too,
Would move beneath his guiding hand
As these great forces do.

The Poet and the Architect

THE poet builds a structure
With the substance of his soul;
Word by word, and line by line
He builds a perfect whole:
A shining thing of living,
Of dreams that will not dim,
A timeless thing that will become
A memorial to him.

The architect does wonders
With wood and brick and stone;
He builds with many helpers,
But all the while—alone—
The poet lifts for ages
A structure set apart
For the solace and the comforting
Of the human heart.

A Darkened Street

THIS little street is still as death tonight,
   The small roofs hover down all mother-
      wise;
No window glows, save one pale wistful light
Marks where a watcher waits with anxious eyes.
The star points tip the eaves with silver mist;
The wind among the hedges goes to keep
Some strange nocturnal vigil, and a tryst
With Life's and Death's dark silent brother—
   Sleep.

Here sleep has wrapped each little house around,
The clamoring heartbeats have been muffled low
Until a breath is but a soundless sound,
And there is nothing left of life to know.
Dear God, thy tired children are asleep—
Watch them lest their slumber grows too deep.

The Essence

THE heart asks often: "What is poetry?
What is its essence? Where can it be
found?"
And strange how vague the answer when we see
It in the new wheat lifting from the ground,
In a loaf of bread, in water from a spring,
Or in a plowshare deep in fertile loam,
In any simple fundamental thing
In constant daily use about a home.

We feel it in the wind among the corn,
We hear it in the dripping of the rain.
If loss of sight or sound makes one forlorn
The scent of apples, ripening down a lane,
Or a leaf fire smoke would be enough to tell
To any seeking one, that he may find
The meaning of the word through sense of smell,
Though he be stricken deaf and dumb and blind.

Ancient Materials

HOW good are all the useful things of earth!
A plow, a mixing bowl, a tended hearth,
An auger and a hammer, saw and plane,
The clear glass of a polished windowpane,
Unvarnished lumber piled for future need—
Oh, all of these are beautiful, indeed:
The implements of labor that men's hands
Have used for centuries throughout all lands;
The ancient tried materials, the wood
And metals that have long been proven good—
These elemental things that came to be
The essence of the earth's great poetry.

While It Is Early

IN THE troubled time which we have called
        "Today,"
    We turn before the dawn to find again
A broken tomb, the great stone rolled away,
And in the shadows, still the hope of man
Waits for our recognition and delight;
Waits for our faith to kindle like a flame
And burn anew with the warm steady light
That we have known—when lo, he speaks our
        name!

"Master," we cry, as did the one of old,
"The night has been so dark, the dawn so late,
Reach out thy hand here in the dusk and hold
Us close to thee, dear Lord, and bid us wait
For the dawn to break across the world and bring
Thy light, thy peace, thy blessed comforting."

Evening at Emmaus

I WISH I had been the household mother there
In the Emmaus home that far-off day.
Simon was bringing home a guest. With care
I would have spread our table its best way.
Sunset, and the Sabbath past, I would
Have gathered from the fields a bit of bloom:
A golden spray of mustard would be good
To brighten up the little darkened room.
With pride I would have placed my loaf of bread
Upon the board: my brown sweet offering;
I would be eager that they be well fed
Who had walked so far that afternoon in spring.

Now they are here, and with another Guest!
He hesitates, then enters—speaks to me.
My heart is beating strangely in my breast,
My eyes are filled with tears—I cannot see—
But why? They sit them down, the grace is said,
The Guest accepts our hospitality.
He lifts his eyes to heaven, breaks the bread,
And suddenly we know that it is He:

The risen Lord! The lifted faces shine,
And nothing through the years could have sufficed
To dim the joy and wonder that was mine
In being one to recognize the Christ.

Since You Are Gone

SINCE you are gone, dear Heart, the days and
    nights
    Are strangely silent. I can scarcely bear
The quiet of the house, the silent rooms,
The absence of your footsteps on the stair.
I miss your voice, your laughter through the halls,
Your presence with me through the twilit hours;
And out of doors the whole world speaks of you
Through murmuring trees, and drooping, whis-
    pering flowers.

And meagerly and slowly go the days
Of this my life that I must still live on
To do the work, that we together planned,
Alone and bravely, now that you are gone.
And though the world has lost its light for me,
And this deep grief is all that I can bear,
I know that Heaven is a nearer place,
Made lovelier far to me since you are there.

Star in the Darkness

THE night was dark with no sign of that
      darkness lifting:
   Lost, bewildered, bereft, I had wandered
far;
Then looking skyward I saw a sudden rifting,
And in the midst of the rift—a silver star:

God's lantern hung for me from the heavenly
      ceiling!
His hand had placed it before my eyes to shine
That I might find my way to the blessed healing
Of assurance and safety. Oh, forever mine
Will be the memory of that one clear light
That guided me out of the darkness of my night.

Red Tree

IF I could dip my pen in blood
To write a poem for this tree,
I could not find a deeper red
With which to work authentically,

A velvet tinged with clearest red,
So dark that one might call it black,
With sunlight shedding a rich glow
Through every veined leaf's gorgeous back.

I think this gum tree must have been
God's special pride the day he made
It stand, breath-taking, beautiful,
A thing of color, light and shade.

He must have mixed the sunset glow
With the dahlia's black-red, then have stood
Watching the tree's dark fires burn,
And smiled—knowing that it was good.

Winter Fields

WINTER has closed the windows, locked the door
    Upon the old tired fields, and now they lie
Asleep—no need to struggle any more
For ardent growth, no need to question why
Rain be withheld, and heat be like a fire,
Or why wild wind and hail should dash them down.
They lie now, past regret and past desire,
Clothed in quietness, miles from any town.

Soon they will waken to another spring.
Faith is a living force within the breast,
And hope, a non-defeated, vibrant thing
That will not let even the old fields rest.
They will arise, with laughter, without fear,
To meet another strange, on-coming year.

Deer at Evening

HALF tame for a while
 Before the guns blaze,
  The deer come down at evening time
Through the soft haze
To scan the roadway skimmed with flying cars.
The wire fences hold no hindering bars
For these, the nimble ones.
Alert they stand outside,
Their pointed ears held high and wide,
Stars in their eyes to match the evening star—
A car appears—they whirl, they leap—
They clear the fence with much good space to
  spare,
And land full twenty feet across the air.
No bird can fly more fleetly winged than they
On their swift way.
One wonders that their slim legs do not crack,
Landing among the rocks and stumps,
But loping back
Into the forest depths they go,
The buck, the doe,
Lost from sight through the gathering night.

The Wild Colt

HIS father and mother never knew a bridle,
          A saddle never touched their quivering
               backs.
That this wild colt is wild, it is no wonder,
As swift and free he follows down the tracks
Where others of his kind have gone before him.
His flaming mane atoss, his head held high,
He lunges for a moment on a mesa:
A golden statue etched against the sky.

What sound is borne to him upon the breezes?
What sight has startled him? Ah, who can know?
As up he rears, then turns as swift as lightning,
And plunges down the slope . . . I watch him go
And marvel that so much of sculptured beauty
Is lost upon this lonely desert place:
A young palomino with the pride of ages
Lettered in gold upon his form, his face.

Sagebrush

TO ANY exile, roaming in far places,
The sudden scent of sagebrush on the air
Brings memories of starlight, warm and
friendly,
Of sunshine goldener than anywhere;
Of some high-mettled horse, the creak of leather,
A coyote's lonesome call across the plains,
The infinite stark silence of the mountains,
The clear sweet silver scent of April rains;
Of high plateaus, of sweeping emerald valleys . . .
These stir the latent longing in the breast
For clean and pungent winds across gray sage-
brush,
For the splendor, glamor, glory of the West.

Mountain Torrent

A LIQUID silver flashes in the torrent
  That tumbles on its bright way to the sea:
  Pure silver mined from wind and rain and
 sunlight,
Glinting, glancing, gliding merrily
Over the mossy stones, the wet dark boulders,
Seeking the light in sparkling silver spray,
Roaring down the heights into the canyons
Upon its wild, delirious, laughing way.

The firs stand with their toetips in the water,
So still that scarce a needled bough is stirred,
Until as sharp as if a cry were uttered—
High on its tip, a teetering scarlet bird
Swings above the water with such beauty,
So amazing there against the canyon wall,
So startling—one wonders at its silence
That is so loud, yet makes no sound at all.

A Voice Rang Out

THE frost came early those November
nights,
The cornstalks withered, and the hills
took fire
From the gold and scarlet of the autumn lights
That burned through painted leaves like fierce
desire.
A partridge drummed, a fox-bark rent the air,
The stockade gates were shut, and none too soon,
The night in that strange region was a lair
For all wild things—the golden harvest moon
Climbed slowly upward . . . "We shall choose,"
they said,
"A special day to render thanks to God."
So on the morrow they had richly spread
Their tables with the good fruits of the sod.

"For these we offer thanks," a voice rang out,
A voice whose echo never has been spent.
Within the new land it became a shout—
A settlement became a Continent;
And men still offer thanks, and pause to pray
As the pilgrims did that first Thanksgiving Day.

We Met the Christ

TODAY as I walked along the road,
    Bearing a far too heavy load,
    I came upon a sorrowing one
Bitterly weeping and undone.
I paused by the roadside there to say
Words that might take his grief away.
I told him the loving Christ had said
That they who mourn shall be comforted;
That he gave his promise we would be blest
If we came to him for our needed rest.

I straightened from habit to shift the pack
I had borne so long on my aching back,
And lo, it was gone, and the tears were dried
On the cheeks of the comrade at my side,
Because each in his peculiar way
Had met the Christ on the road that day.

Autumn Fires

THE early frost has not yet quenched the
　　fires
　　That burn their fierce paths through the
autumn days
Where the scarlet creeper's flame, and the
　　brilliant haze
Of maples burn on hills, and the hot haze
Of sumac sweeps across the valley sod.
The smoke of asters still is heavy where
The wind-fanned color of the goldenrod
Is a conflagration on the startled air.

And I shall walk among them, I shall find
A fire to warm me by, a flame to keep
Within my heart when, summer left behind,
The days and nights grow cold, and snow is deep.
When all the gypsy-kindled fires will turn
To ashes on the hills, my fire will burn.

If Christmas Be Kept

IF CHRISTMAS be kept a splendid shining
    thing,
  Sacred and holy in the hearts of men;
If there be selfless gifts that we can bring
To the poor and needy, truly never again
Need we be quite bereft, though ills betide,
And dangers threaten us: for there will be
A heavenly brightness moving by our side,
And hope will spring in hearts eternally.

The Light of the world is centered in the hour
That gave the Christ Child to the waiting earth.
His star still blooms—a radiant silver flower
As a glorious sign and symbol of his birth.
If men keep shining, steadfast faith in him,
They can walk the earth by a light that will not
    dim.

In the Church of the Holy Sepulcher

HERE they have gathered through the
        starlit night
    To worship where the infant Christ had
lain.
The tall, white candles burn. One blazing star
Hangs like liquid fire above the plain.
They come, long lines of pilgrims from the world,
Drawn by some inward urge, some desperate
        need:
The royal rich, the pitifully poor,
Seeking the bread on which their hearts can feed.
I watch them there—a lowly peasant comes
Bent with many sorrows, many years;
He lays his cheek against the altar's ledge,
And 'tis as if his mother dried his tears.
I see a small boy kiss his hands and reach
To lay that kiss where once the Child had been;
And here a young priest kneels to form a cross,
And plead to God for mercy for men's sin.
And now a sobbing woman stoops to place
Her quivering lips upon the altar stone.
One stumbles blindly, reaching out to touch

The place that held a friend that he had known.
And still they come, the pilgrims through the
    night,
The young, the old, the sad, the starry-eyed,
Seeking the Holy Sepulcher to have
Their nameless thirst and hunger satisfied.
The world from whence they came has not
    sufficed
To still the heart's deep longing for the Christ.

To a Lady in Black

YOU are a poem, and you are a song,
You are lovely in your quiet grace:
Your eyes are gray with shadows worn
for long,
And yet no shadow mars your tranquil face.
Something there is in you—all still and white—
That is like clean snow upon a distant hill.
It reminds me of a moonlit field at night:
This look of yours that is so white and still.

You who wear black for your near precious dead
Have found a path of peace through your deep
pain;
Wild grief has swept you, yet you lift your head
As a flower lifts its proud head after rain.
Although life casts its shadows in your eyes,
Your sorrow makes you beautiful and wise.

Organic and Choir

THE tapered golden pipes of the organ
    climb
    Ceilingward, their tubes adrip with notes
Rising and falling as far faint bells chime;
And the lifted columns of the singers' throats
Give forth an anthem's high insistent call,
And gleam above the surplices they wear.
The music seeks the rafters there to fall
Like incense sifting brightly on the air.

"The Power and the Glory," high and higher
The voices sound in full melodic praise.
The sun through colored windows strikes a fire
Across the gold pipes, and the slanting rays
Pick out the hands that move across the keys,
And a face uplifted in white ecstasy . . .
While music, forcing the listeners to their knees,
Links close this hour to Eternity.

"Our Father"

SOMETIMES, dear Lord, two words are all
      we need
    In a prayer that will be heard.
As a little frightened child calls through the dark
One importuning word,
And his earthly parent hastens to his side
To comfort and to cheer,
So we may call, "Our Father," through the dark;
And suddenly as near
As hands or feet or breathing, you will be
Beside us, waiting there,
Knowing our need before our tongues can shape
A further word of prayer,
Willing to answer. O our gracious Lord,
How often men have cried
In every tongue these importuning words,
And you were by their side,
Needing no further voicing; and their hearts
Were stilled and satisfied.

The Harpist

HER fingers swept the strings, and suddenly
A host of golden butterflies took wing—
Outward and upward, shaking the startled air,
And the waiting hearts of those who were listen-
ing.
There was color and light in those impinging
wings,
The weight of sunlight and of crystal dew,
The burning orange of an autumn flower,
The gauze wings dripping silver as they flew.
The music ran like laughter out to meet
Life's heady rapture in a song set free—
It climbed the heights to shout its singing joy,
In a quick release of wild sweet ecstasy.

Unuttered Faith

THE farmer plowing through ashes
  After the fiery drought,
  Perhaps may not be voicing
Prayer and praise with his mouth;
But his is a faith as shining
As the early morning sun—
Watch how straight and certain
His upturned furrows run;
See him move unhindered
In the rising pillar of dust;
If there be food for next year
Plow he must.
So forward he drives his bright shares
Through the parched and yielding sod,
Thus showing a clear, though unvoiced,
Faith in God.

Walking in Rain

TO BE young and strong with the wild wind
        beating
    Hard on the roof and the windowpane,
Would be a signal to be going
Out in the driving wind and rain.
Cloaked and shod in glistening rubber,
Who is afraid of the needling sting
Of silver arrows on face and shoulders—
Walking in rain is a glorious thing!

Breathing the clean air, breaking the silver
Slant of the rain in its downward flight,
To be part of the wild day's heady laughter,
To be one with the moving shadow and light
Is to have a sense of release and freedom,
Is to take on the feel of power and might.

Compassion

SUFFERING with another," thus the word
"Compassion" is defined. O Heart grown
sad
Through some strange troubled hour, recall the
Lord
And the tender swift compassion that he had
For all he met upon his earthly road:
The troubled ones, the hurt, the blind, the lame,
And that he reached to lift the heavy load
From the bodies and the hearts of all who came.

"Suffering with another." I am sure
The same Lord, with the same swift healing
power,
Still has compassion on us that can cure
The ills of earth through any darkened hour.
His hand is still outstretched to bring relief
To all earth's pilgrims as we travel on,
And I have found—almost beyond belief—
My sorrow easing, and the old pain gone.

To a Christian Doctor

(To M.A.P.)

SOMETHING of God is in your gentle
touch,
Something divine is in the hope you give
The weary suffering ones who need so much
That touch, that hope, the impetus to live.
Faithfully you answer every call
Though worn you be by many quick demands,
And skillfully you render aid to all
Who seek relief from your outgiving hands.

God bless you through the days that are to be.
May he give you wisdom, may he give you
strength
To serve mankind in your community
So miraculously, so well, until at length—
Some far eternal day—the voice of One,
The greatest of all physicians, cries, "Well done!"

When Sleep Is a Stranger to My Eyes

SOMETIMES when sleep is a stranger to
          my eyes
     I turn back to an old forgotten lane
And cross a stile to where a meadow lies
Deep in the summer dusk, and there again,
Hand in hand I walk with one long gone,
With one, O much beloved! The meadow grass
Lies bruised beneath our feet as we move on,
And the new moon marks our shadows as we
          pass.

Sweet is the fragrance—gentle the early star
Whose wistful face looks from the western sky,
And dear the hand on mine—oh, lost and far
Is the meadow and the moon, and the faint cry
Of a late bird flying homeward to its nest . . .
O Love, come back—come back that I may rest!

Spanish Song

OUT of the night silvered with many a star
There comes the sudden throb of a steel
guitar,
And a haunting voice lifts high, and sobs and
sings
A song filled with the ache of vanished springs.
It trembles delicately upon the air . . .
What is it, ecstasy or wild despair
That it awakes? "*La Golondrina* . . ." Hark!
A senorita's voice rings through the dark
Like bells—a man's voice joins as one,
Filled with the golden warmth of the tropic sun,
And the hot blaze of flowers shot with light.
The music rises, breaks against the night,
And now "*Cielito Lindo* . . ." strange that throats
Can hold the rapture of those liquid notes!
Strange that gliding steel upon bright strings
Has power to lift one up on unseen wings,
And that two dark-skinned singers with their art
Can kindle a leaping fire within the heart!

Anomaly

LOVE is a strange anomaly:
It is as fragile as a vine,
It is as strong as the strongest tree,
It is human, and divine.

O tender plant, I shall not touch
One delicate tendril, one bright spray,
Lest handling you overmuch
I tear your clinging life away.

And O strong, splendid, lovely tree,
So tall you are, so deep your roots,
You quench my thirst, you shelter me,
You feed my hunger with your fruits.

So frail, so strong, so much a part
Of life itself—love waits me there:
A strong tree, sheltering my heart,
A vine that needs my tenderest care.

Ocean Sunset

THIS is an hour of misty light to carry
    Into the winter, into the cold and dark,
    A sunset hour glowing like an ember
That had been lit by some live flying spark.
The shore, a moment ago, a golden splendor,
Is reddened by the flame that sweeps the land;
The waves are bright with scarlet foam; the
    shadows
Are luminous that race along the sand.

Even the waving grasses of the marshland
Are washed with carmine color, and afar
The weathered lighthouse wears a silver luster
Tipped as it is by the early evening star.
Overhead the sea gulls swoop—the herons
Cry raucously among the reedy sedge,
And oh, the startling rose-pink of the plumage
Of a lone flamingo at the water's edge!

Two Old Friends

TWO old friends are sitting together
Sipping their tea. The autumn weather
Requires the first fire's flickering glow.
Around them the shelved books, row on row,
Catch the wavering light and hold
The glimmer of titles etched in gold.
Brasses gleam and the rubbed woods shine.
Old worn fabrics that once were fine
Surround them as they sit at tea
In accustomed, upright dignity.

Above the tinkle of spoon and cup,
They talk of old days as they sup:
Of friends who are gone a long, long while,
Of the beaux they had, and they sit and smile,
Remembering this, and remembering that,
And the clock ticks on as they sit and chat.
It nibbles away—the hour ends—
So little time left for two old friends!

The Brave Doing of the Common Task

THIS shall I covet for my life's brief day.
These are the simple things for which I
ask:
A quiet goodness as I go my way,
And the brave doing of the common task—
The common task—how courageous is the heart
That meets with patient grace the day-long toil!
Many there are who staunchly go their way
Dealing with shop or home, or stubborn soil,
Meeting life with a calm serenity,
With faith and trust that no ill wind can shake.
I pray this spirit may be given me
That out of a commonplace day I can make
Bright hours of beauty, hours of shining peace,
Where all tumult and clamoring will cease.

I Wish I Knew

SOMETIMES when long shadows lie
Across the waving glinting grass,
And over your grave the soft winds pass
Caressingly as they go by,
I look across the years and see
One afternoon when we two walked
Among the quiet graves and talked
Of death and of Eternity;
Of life, and what it meant to live.
Death seemed a thing too far away
From our young hearts that summer day,
And life too high a price to give.

But awed, we wondered what the dead
Knew then of things we did not know:
"The changing and the mystery
Of death—all these they know," we said.
And now today a shadow lies
Across your grave, and I am here,
Wondering what this brief year
Has been to you in Paradise.

You know so much I cannot know,
You see so much I cannot see,
And understand the things that we
Were questioning, yet could not know . . .
Call back—how does it fare with you?
I wish I knew! I wish I knew!